"I'd rather see a rhino charge at me
That way I have a chance at winning. And now you can too.
-Pat Croce, best-selling author and serial entrepreneur

"I have spent time with some of the biggest names in the music and entertainment industry, yet not one of them has ever had the effect on me that Dave Magrogan has. Dave can find the bright spot in any dark cloud. Dave has turned my lowest moments into positive experiences. He's the best friend I have...and the shortest."
-John DeBella, Radio host, TV personality and infamous creator of the WMMR Morning Zoo in Philadelphia

"Inspirational...The book guides you to focus on your attitudes, positive thoughts, failures, values, philosophies and dreams to develop concrete, meaningful goals. Just what I needed - a kick start to CHARGE FORWARD."
-Sandy Knapp, partner in Gawthrop Greenwood law firm, business owner, and busy working mom

"Compelling, motivational, and wholly practical. Dave Magrogan is a master."
-Anthony Gold, CEO, Healthy Humans, President, Open Solutions Alliance, Guinness Book of World Records holder

"Attitude. Attitude. Attitude. Dave proves that when you have the right plan in place, multiply it by positive energy, positive attitude and add a dose of passion, magical things happen."
-Kimberly Brumbaugh, Founder of Brumbaugh Wealth Management Group, philanthropist, busy mother of three, and champion advocate for autistic children

"Do It Rhino Style is truly inspirational. The book offers profound insight from the mind of a man who has dared to dream big. It provides a pragmatic and simple approach to help people realize their dreams and potential."

-Greg Olive, CFO, Volvo Information Technology NA

"When it comes to success, the Rhino is in CHARGE. Follow Dave's goal achieving formula so you don't get run over by mistake!"

-John Sacharok, CEO, Golden Valley Farms

"Dave Magrogran, serial entrepreneur and motivational mogul, opens his kimono to share his practical advice with the masses!"

-Diego Calderin, President & Founder, Anexinet Corp

"Everyone wants to be a part of something big. The difference with Dave is that he makes you want to CAUSE something big, not just be a part of it, and here therein lies the difference."

-Michael Karwic, Sudden Wealth Advisor
and Certified Financial Planner

"In five short and easy to understand...and follow for yourself...chapters, Magrogan has a laid out his path to personal and financial success. It's worked for him and will work for anyone. Everyone looking to change their life for the better should read this book, implement the ideas, and...Charge!"

-Steven Smolinsky, author and speaker, founder Conversation on
Networking, President Benari LTD, Profession Faculty and
Africa Manager Wharton Global Consulting Practicum

In six short years, Dave Magrogan took Kildare's from an unknown start up pub to being recognized as the 7th best Irish pub in the world. He is CEO of a $25 million dollar empire—including Rhino Living Training & Consulting Group, Kildare's, Doc Magrogan's Oyster House, Harvest, and Mas Mexicali Cantina. He also serves as president of the Southeastern Pennsylvania Division of Two Men and a Truck Moving Company and helped launch Pat Croce's Rum Barrel in Key West and various other businesses.

Dave has been a finalist in the 2006 and 2007 Ernst & Young Entrepreneur of the year competition. He was also recognized by the Philadelphia Business Journal as one of the region's "40 Under 40" in 2007 and by the Chester County Chamber of Business and Industry as its 2007 Entrepreneur of the Year. He also received the Small Business Administration's Entrepreneurial Success Award for 2008, and Kildare's Irish Pub was ranked 26th in Philadelphia's Fastest growing 100 Companies. Not bad for someone 36 years of age!

DO IT RHINO STYLE

MAGROGAN'S METHOD TO RAPID GOAL ACHIEVEMENT

DAVE MAGROGAN

WITH *MOLLY NECE*

DO IT RHINO STYLE
Magrogan's Method
to Rapid Goal Achievement™

ISBN: 978-0-615-34094-4

Printed in the United States of America
By Bentley Graphics
www.bentleygraphics.com

INTRODUCTION

This book was written in true rhino style. It started with a rush of inspiration while I was brainstorming how I could help my oldest daughter Ivy through a critical transition in her life. Ivy had moved from her mother's home to my home and was about to start a new school. It was a fresh start and I wanted her to not focus on the negative events of the past year, but rather focus on all the opportunities that were in her future.

I started to pull together all of the pieces from my Rhino Living keynotes and website, Rhino Action Sheets, weekly e-mails and blogs, and my corporate training materials I use with all my employees and outside clients. What I realized is I was creating Ivy's Rapid Goal Achievement System—one designed just for her! I bought her all the tools she needed to sit down and get excited about her future, her dreams and her goals.

On November 27th, a force of Rhino inspiration hit me. Why should I only be doing this for Ivy? Why not share it with the world? People at all stages of their life could benefit from 'this system' and it's a proven system that works! By Dec 1st this book was complete with the help of my amazing, energetic, Rhino Living business partner, Molly.

What started out as a way to help my daughter get refocused, passionate, and excited about her dreams, quickly evolved into the simplest, fastest and most effective book on how to achieve your goals faster than you could ever imagine!

This goal setting book was developed from years of real life and academic principles which I use everyday in the 15 different businesses I own and operate. That's why some call me "The Rhino of Monetizing Dreams." You really can achieve your goals faster than you think is possible. This book is a prime example of Rapid Goal Achievement™! It was written in two days and published in two weeks—just in time to be the perfect gift for the holidays and to ring in the New Year with a fresh perspective and a Rhino Living vision towards achieving your goals!

Charge!
Dave

"The longer I live, the more I realize the impact of attitude on life. Attitude, to me, is more important than facts. It is more important than the past, the education, the money, than circumstances, than failure, than successes, than what other people think or say or do. It is more important than appearance, giftedness or skill. It will make or break a company... a church... a home. The remarkable thing is we have a choice everyday regarding the attitude we will embrace for that day. We cannot change our past... we cannot change the fact that people will act in a certain way. We cannot change the inevitable. The only thing we can do is play on the one string we have, and that is our attitude. I am convinced that life is 10% what happens to me and 90% of how I react to it. And so it is with you... we are in charge of our attitudes."

-Charles Swindoll

CONTENTS

CONTENTS

CHAPTER ONE
CLEAR THE MENTAL CLUTTER

Congratulations!

You have taken a very important first step in taking control of your life. Today you start to become a happy, enthusiastic, and positive Rhino! You can achieve your goals if you believe you can and if you charge full steam ahead. All success starts with a positive mental attitude. Without a positive attitude you will never be able to deal with all the issues that arise on the charge to your dreams. Starting today, wake up every day and choose to have a positive attitude. It's the foundation of success. There are few things you get to control 100 percent in your life—your attitude is one of them. Having a clear vision of your most important goals, combined with a positive attitude, makes you an unstoppable gigantic Rhino on the fast track to success. Let's get started!

You become what you think about

Whatever you think about with emotion and energy you will bring about in your life. Where you are today is the sum of the beliefs and actions you have taken over the past several years. Your dominant thoughts work deep into your subconscious mind, and once there, they go to work to bring about who you are and what lies in your future. Where you are today is a sum of your past. As a Rhino, you need to embrace a positive attitude and make sure to have positive big dreams for your future.

Today you are experiencing your dominant thoughts of your past. Tomorrow you can experience the dominant thoughts of your new way of positive thinking.

This is why you need to think BIG! RHINO BIG! If today you start making one of your dominant thoughts to become a millionaire, you will uncover ways to become a millionaire. If you take action, in five years you could be that millionaire! When I opened my first Kildare's I told everyone, including my staff, that we are going to be in the top ten Irish pubs in the world. Each staff meeting I would reinforce the top ten goal. Five years later, we accomplished our goal! If you think small and hope in five years you are making a little more money and your car is paid off, then in five years that is exactly what will happen. What you think about and believe with emotion you will bring about! Don't believe it? Here's a little proof! At age 6 I built my own lemonade stand. Yep!

I opened my very first pub when I was only 6 years old. I look at the picture of me in the lemonade stand everyday in my office to remember how power-ful one's thoughts can be! What you think today will become your future! Yep that's me…

My wife Shannon was recently featured as Rhino Living's Top Rhino because she took first place in her age group in the US Triathlon Finals in California. In addition, she recently returned from a trip to Australia where she came in 9th in the World Triathlon Championships! Can you guess what picture is hanging in our home gym? It's a big blown up picture from the Philadelphia Inquirer from 1990 where Shannon at age 15, as an unknown underdog, won the Penn Relays. See, this stuff really works!

If you have children you must be thinking, "What can I do to help them reach their goals in such a powerful way?" While in Australia, Grady, our son, got a picture taken wearing his mom's Team US Triathlon uniform. Only time will tell what path he will take, but if he's in the Olympics one day, it will be no surprise!

Remember to inspire yourself, your friends, and your kids. Negative thoughts and actions will accumulate in your life and will only attract negative results. Positive, big ideas will result in a big, fun, positive life! You hold the power over your own thoughts, and you can be a source of great inspiration for those around you. Part of being a Rhino and leaving others in the pasture of mediocrity is to take personal responsibility for your actions. You own your attitude, control your thoughts and you certainly create your own realty. Nobody else can control these things. You have the power to take the state of your own mind and direct it to the end results you desire. Your boss can't stop you, your spouse can't stop you and your past cannot stop you.

You are a giant, positive, energetic RHINO—nothing can stop you once you determine what you want! Decide today to stop blaming others for where you are and what you have become. Take the time to clear the mental clutter, think positive, visualize your ideal future and start letting your subconscious mind take control you will become what you think about!

Where you will be next month, next year and in five years is completely up to you. By controlling your thoughts and dreaming big, you can transform your life and live your dreams! Think negative, self damaging thoughts, you will live it. Think BIG POSITIVE RHINO thoughts and you will live a BIG FUN EXCITING life! It really works!

Take the Truth or Lie challenge

List the five most common things people have said about you over the years. Beside each comment, write "truth" or "lie." The first step is to start to clear the mental clutter and get to the truth who you are and who you want to become.

1

2

3

4

5

Mind map your past and predict your future

A mind map is a diagram used to represent words, ideas,

or other items linked to and arranged around a central key thought, idea or situation. Mind maps are also used to generate, visualize, structure, and classify ideas. To help you clear the mental clutter, I want you to look back in your past to see how you can mind map how you got to where you are today. When you get into "Chapter Three of Writing Your Goals," I want you to remember what you did to chart your past because you did to chart your past because you can chart your future using the same mind mapping tool. Here is a sample of one of one of my client's mind maps. Utilizing the power of mind mapping helps you and others solve problems make decisions and chart your future success!

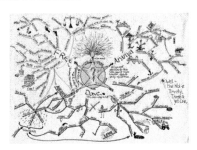

Failure is all in your head

Benjamin Franklin said it best. "To try and fail is at least to learn. To fail to try is to suffer the loss of what might have been." Most people fail before they take the first step. They believe they will fail so they don't even try. They fear criticism so they don't charge boldly in the direction of their dreams. Most failure is the failure of a person to take the risk and the challenge to create something better. If you are a Rhino (and we all have a little Rhino in us), you need to understand that standing in the field of safety and mediocrity is no way to live. Giving up your life in exchange for safety and security is to not have lived at all. Do you fear failure? If so, why? What is there to fear?

I'm going to challenge you to change your perspective and "fear not!" I highly recommend Susan Jeffers' book "Feel the Fear and Do It Anyway." You need to change your perspective about failure. Remember, life is 10 percent what happens to you and 90 percent how you react to it. Simply changing how you view "failure" can change your life.

Failure is a very positive thing. It teaches you how to do it better next time, increases your skills, increases your knowledge and improves your perspective. Failure gives you wisdom—the wisdom to make better and more efficient decisions in the future. Many people look at failure as some permanent state that will forever define who they are. The fear of failure at work, in sports, at home, or in the public eye prevent most people from living their dreams.

Change your perspective from seeing failure as a permanent, destructive force to a positive learning experience that is essential on the path to success. You will not be a perfect success at everything you attempt. Success in any field comes from doing some things right and doing some things wrong. The final product is success created by the ups and downs, the positives and negatives and the modified actions created by small hurdles—also known as "failures"—along the way. All big success is achieved by failing forward.

You might fear the thought of "what will people say if I fail?" Who cares! Seriously, do you really care what others say as they stand in the field criticizing you for taking a chance? Remember, people with grazing tendencies are scared to leave the herd and live their dreams. You are creating the life YOU desire, the life YOU want to live. Not a life justified by others! If you fail, it is a very good sign. It means you are moving forward. You are challenging your intelligence and you are taking chances. If you fail, it means you are not standing still in the pasture! People will always remember your success more than your failures. And people that constantly hang on to your failures are doing it to justify their own lack of action.

It's good to celebrate your GIANT 6,000 POUND FAILURE! Guess what? I am a giant rhino-sized failure! I have failed thousands of times and I expect to fail a million more times in this adventure called life. You are reading this and becoming a Rhino because of my failures. I have faced adversity and I continue to charge. I have taken failure and made it a positive and I have gained tremendous knowledge to help you achieve success faster because of the information I learned through my own failures.

When I was a chiropractor, I would convert 3 out of 10 new patients to a lifetime patient. Essentially, if I had a negative outlook, I failed to convert 7 out of 10 patients to become my ideal patient. But by converting 3 patients per week to lifetime care, I built the largest practice in Pennsylvania. 3 wins a week was all it took to see 800 patients a week and build a very successful practice. It's all about positive reframing...with everything!

In the restaurant business, I have opened 14 restaurants and closed 3. What did I learn in closing 3 locations?

When you have a bad location, close it quickly and don't spend time, money and energy trying to save the wrong spot. These restaurant failures taught me how to better investigate locations, obtain better financing options, perform better staff training and most of all, that it was okay to admit you picked a bad spot or the wrong staff and let go of the sinking ship.

Pride, embarrassment, and fear of public failure kept some of these locations open a year too long. When you have failed at a project, a dream or a goal, and you know it's time to move on and try something else, do it! Follow your gut. If it is a temporary setback, a lesson, or hurdle, keep charging. If you know in your heart something is over, don't worry about the public, and don't worry about the negative naysayers. Do what is right in your heart and your gut.

Alexander Graham Bell said that "Sometimes we stare so long at a door that is closing that we see too late the one that is open." The bottom line is you must fail to succeed. As a Rhino, you need to embrace failure and learn from it. It is an important element of success and you cannot succeed without it. With every goal you set, you will encounter failure along the way. Expect it, welcome it and learn from it. Share the knowledge you gain from failures and help other Rhinos bravely face the failures in their life.

Assess your charging traits and grazing tendencies

Identify a specific challenging situation that you recently encountered in your life. Place a check mark beside each of the 12 behaviors in the two categories that best described how you approached the situation. Total the two columns and assess what you did well and what you will do differently charging forward!

My Charging Traits: Behaviors that would keep me on my charge and seeking opportunities.

1. Admitted life can be challenging and I created every outcome.
2. Believed I control every outcome of my life.
3. Decided life unfolds according to my thoughts, beliefs, and actions.
4. Clearly identified what wasn't working in my life.
5. Admitted my problems were a direct result of my choices.
6. Was entirely ready to solve my problems.
7. Looked for ways I could solve my problems and surrounded myself with positive people who could help me.
8. Acknowledged my thoughts, beliefs, and actions led to my experiences.
9. Shifted my focus to a better-feeling thought in all aspects of my life.
10. Continued to examine how my thoughts, beliefs, and actions created my outcomes.
11. Sought every opportunity to learn from my challenges, improve my skills, and stay out of other people's lives.
12. Having experienced freedom and empowerment as a result of this process, I practiced taking 100% responsibility in all my affairs.

My Grazing Tendencies: Behaviors that would take me off my charge and keep me grazing in the field.

1. Thought it was NOT my fault!

2. Believed outcomes in my life were not in my control.
3. Decided nothing goes my way.
4. Clearly identified why other people's lives weren't effective.
5. Admitted my problems would be solved or at least lessened, if people, situations, and things were different.
6. Was entirely willing to turn my problems over to someone else.
7. Looked for other people to solve my problems.
8. Cited a list of hardships, disappointments, and wrongdoings done to me as justifications of my actions.
9. Mentally replayed hardships, disappointments, and wrongdoings done to me over and over again.
10. Continued to provide evidence how my outcomes were out of my control
11. Sought every opportunity to point out other people's mistakes and hoped to witness them "get theirs."
12. Having experienced such woes, I freely shared them wherever I went and with whomever I met.

RAPID GOAL ACHIEVEMENTS

- ❑ I became what I thought about. It's the Law of Belief!
- ❑ I took the 'Truth and Lie Challenge' and cleared the mental clutter.
- ❑ I mapped out my future through mind-mapping.
- ❑ I experienced first hand that failing forward is a positive thing.
- ❑ I strengthened my charging traits and weakened by grazing tendencies.
- ❑ I am focused on passions and eliminated obstacles.
- ❑ I am dedicated to living and charging with a positive Rhino attitude.
- ❑ I went to RhinoLiving.com and signed up for my weekly Rhino motivation.

"MY IMAGINATION CREATES MY REALITY."
-Walt Disney

CHAPTER TWO
GET YOUR SELF IMAGE ON BOARD

The man in the mirror

Henry David Thoreau said that "The world is but a canvas to the imagination." When Michael Jackson died, it seemed that the news coverage would never end. CNN continued to break into important news stories with the latest exclusive details about his death, latest rehearsal, the drugs found in his home and the constant replays of his memorial service.

Americans are consumed with celebrities and it doesn't appear it will ever change. The rise, fall, and rise again trajectory of being a celebrity can be brutal to watch. "Jacko the Wacko" has gone from a "perverted sicko" to "musical genius" again. In life, Michael was abused, arrested, and ridiculed. In death, he is a genius we will miss forever. This is the cycle of almost all celebrities. Few can break from the love/hate cycle with the American public. Jon and Kate, America's favorite family, were scorned for every step they took. Britney Spears couldn't buy a cup of coffee without scandal, and the list goes on.

It is the sad path of fame, but what saddens me more is the "man in the mirror." The delicate and shattered self-image most of these celebrities hide with drugs, alcohol, money and toys is what ultimately destroys them in the end. Regardless of fame or money, who you are on the inside will ultimately determine your success or failure.

Michael Jackson was destined for self-sabotage and self-destruction because the "man in the mirror" was still an 9 year old boy abused by his father, longing for the joy of childhood and unhappy with his features. No amount of fame, wealth or pills would fix the negative self-image he saw every time he looked in the mirror. He was never able to put his past behind him. He was never able to look forward into the future without being limited by his childhood damage. No matter what financial happiness, fame and success MJ enjoyed, the negative image he saw every time he looked in the mirror made him unable to achieve happiness. Even the 30 million dollar Neverland ranch could not bring Michael's childhood back. It only brought him more pain and misfortune.

Recently I watched "Walk the Line" again, the Johnny Cash story....great movie! As you travel through his life story, you see that a tragic event in his youth and a destructive father continued to damage him throughout his life. All through his life he went through battles with depression, drugs, and alcohol in an attempt to deal with the first 12 years of his life. His father had convinced him he was not good enough and he should not even be alive. Johnny Cash believed this for most of his adult life. Had June Carter not been there to show him what he really looked like in the mirror, he would never have survived.

Now you see it, now you don't

What do you see when you look in the mirror? Do you see a view of yourself that is distorted because of your past? Are you holding on to your childhood and reliving bad memories preventing happiness in the present?

The level of your success in life will be controlled by your self-image. You need to put your past behind you and start to charge at the future with unbridled optimism. The best events have not happened to you yet and the past can never be relived. You can only achieve goals consistent with your self-image. If you believe you can sell 10 million dollars in real estate this year, you can. If you believe you are only good enough to sell 5 million, you are right again.

When you look in the mirror, do you see your amazing talents, gifts and potential, or do you see all the negative experiences and comments from your past? Looking in the mirror and constantly seeing your past will keep you firmly rooted there.

Don't allow your subconscious mind overpower your ability to achieve

I was told a story by a speaker while in chiropractic school. I never verified if it was true, but it goes a long way in explaining how we live in self-imposed comfort zones, imposed by negative self-images and beliefs.

A tiger was having a new habitat built in a zoo in the United States. While the new habitat was under construction, the tiger spent most of his time in a very small cage. The tiger would constantly pace the perimeter of the cage. Funding for the new habitat fell short, and as a result, the tiger spent substantially more time than planned in this small confining space. When the tiger's new habitat was finally completed, and the tiger was released into the habitat. Guess what he did? For weeks this tiger just kept pacing the same perimeter he had walked for the past year. The cage was gone, the bars were gone and the tiger was free to roam in his beautiful, new environment, but he was still in a prison of his own mind. His mind was so confined, limited and locked into the cage that his mind could not see the beauty and freedom of his new habitat.

I bet you can identify with that story. How many times have you made yourself a prisoner in your own mind and prevented yourself from taking exciting new opportunities because you were still living in the limits from your past? Cut the cord! When a baby elephant is being trained to be a circus animal, the first thing the trainer does is place a heavy chain to its ankle and attach it to a stake in the ground. The little elephant tried to break free, but he quickly becomes "conditioned" that it is impossible. As the elephant ages, it learns that any rope tied to his ankle will prevent him from being free. When the elephant is full grown and weighs several tons, a simple rope wrapped around a small spike in the ground will crush all of his hopes and dreams of being able to run free. He will be a prisoner of a rope that has no real hold on him.

The lifetime of negative, self-limiting beliefs you hold in your subconscious mind are even more powerful than the little rope holding an elephant back. Every time you feel the self-limiting beliefs holding you back, picture the elephant or the tiger and remember you are a 6,000 pound Rhino and absolutely nothing can stop you!

Take the Law of Averages Test

Because of what you see in the mirror, like attracts like. We've all heard of this before and now it has been proven that we are the average of the top ten people we spend the most time with. Below, list those top ten people. Beside their name, indicate which people have charging traits (C) and which ones have grazing tendencies (G) 75% of the time. Everyone has some grazing tendencies. It's important that we know how to manage them and surround ourselves with those who spend most of their time charging. See chapter one for descriptions.

If you couldn't come up with ten people, that's your first goal. Your second goal is to replace those people with grazing tendencies, with those who have charging traits. Build your Rhino Dream Team!

1	6
2	7
3	8
4	9
5	10

Uncovering true Rhinos

It is during times of great adversity that your false friends fall by the wayside and our true enemies show their face. As a Rhino, you need to remember the path to success in any venture, business, school, or life will have its peaks and valleys. You will have times when you are on your "A" game and it appears you can do no wrong. People will cheer you on, friends will surround you and people will sing your praises. Then there will be times when you hit a valley, a bad cycle or a few bumps in the road. It is then that your true friends and supporters will show themselves.

It's tough being a Rhino and at times can be lonely as you build your Rhino Dream Team. As a Rhino you need to remember that you will experience success and failures as your charge towards the things that are important to you. You will be leading with new thoughts, new actions and new beliefs. This will make you stand out from the crowd. At times you will have a team of Rhinos around you and at times you will be standing all alone. You will be the only one willing to fight the fight, the only one committed to achieving your goal no matter what, and the only one willing to lose it all. Everyone around you may have lost faith in you—your friends, your family, your colleagues, your bankers, your boss—and they will lose faith in your vision. But you are a Rhino! You can charge and achieve your goals regardless of the negative people, circumstances and cycles. When the going gets tough you will look around and often see nobody there to support you. They lack the commitment, the strength, and the will to persevere during the difficult times. But you, Rhino, must charge on! Success in any venture or project is based on your ability to persist and believe in yourself even when everyone else has abandoned you.

Be wary of the people with grazing tendencies hiding in Rhino's clothing. It's easy for people to ride your coat tails and pat you on the back when you are winning. When you are experiencing success, making progress and winning key victories, there will be lots of "wanna be" Rhinos there singing the company line and "committed" to the big vision! But when the failures start, when the road gets difficult, and when total failure seems possible, the fear will set in. They will get frazzled, lose their commitment and start to disappear one by one. Their strong "Rhino" attitude will give way to the grazing tendencies of doubt, blame and pity. Soon, the very Rhino they followed and praised will be the root of all their problems. The decisions they supported in the past when everything was going well will now be the "bad" decisions of the Rhino leader they encouraged. They will eventually fade away from the company, the project, or your life. And yes, they will blame you, the Leader Rhino, for the misfortunes that come their way. They will not accept personal responsibility, nor understand that success has its ups and downs and will try to tear you down.

The good news is that during times of great turmoil, the true Rhinos rise to the occasion. Just when the negative people are ganging up on you…just as you start to feel alone in the world… and just as your dreams seem to be vanishing in front of you, a miraculous thing will happen. New true Rhinos of your Rhino Dream Team will appear. They will admire your persistence, your courage and your willingness to charge full steam ahead even when the world is closing in around you. As the negative people in your life drop like flies because success is too hard, because they fear failure and because they have lost faith, new energetic Rhinos will appear. They will be there during the rough times to help you, they will add experience, and they will fill you with new energy and revitalize your dream!

The good news is that without failures, you will never know who your false friends are. You will never know who is really committed to your vision and dream until the road becomes difficult. Then and only then will people show their true colors. It is then that the "wanna be" Rhinos take off their Rhino clothes and show their real grazing traits. It is then that fear becomes the motivator rather than faith. It is then from out of nowhere new Rhinos will arrive on the scene and help create the next success. Some of these new Rhinos have been there all along and because others have disappeared. There is now room to move them up on the company ladder or add them to your inner Rhino circle so they can help you fulfill your mission and vision in life.

"The definition of success--To laugh much; to win respect of intelligent persons and the affections of children; to earn the approbation of honest critics and endure the betrayal of false friends; to appreciate beauty; to find the best in others; to give one's self; to leave the world a little better, whether by a healthy child, a garden patch, or a redeemed social condition; to have played and laughed with enthusiasm, and sung with exultation; to know even one life has breathed easier because you have lived--this is to have succeeded." -Ralph Waldo Emerson

Live passionately. Align your values with your dreams

A Rhino's top five core values typically stands the test of time and do not change throughout life. When there is misalignment between a Rhino's values and a goal, they can become frustrated, bored and unhappy in their Rhino Life. Before setting goals, it is important to identify your core values so charging Rhinos don't end up grazing and miserable!

It is also recommended that you have your family and friends complete the Rhino Values Game tool! You will begin to experience stronger relationships and begin to understand what people value in their everyday life.

Place a checkmark beside the 15 values you consider important to you. Of those 15, select ten that are significantly more important to you. Of those ten, circle your top five core rhino values. It's natural to struggle a little in the process of identifying your top five values.

1. Family Happiness
2. Health
3. Recognition (status, recognition from others)
4. Advancement (classes, sports, leadership positions)
5. Loyalty
6. Adventure (new challenges)
7. Involvement (being involved with others)
8. Self Respect (pride)
9. Competitiveness (winning, taking risks)
10. Friendship (close relationships with others)
11. Power (influence over others)
12. Order (stability, conformity)
13. Integrity (honest, standing up for oneself)
14. Creativity (imaginative, innovative)
15. Helpfulness (helping others, improving society)
16. Wealth (getting rich, making money)

17. Wisdom (discovering, new knowledge)
18. Economic Security
19. Responsibility (accountable for results)
20. Inner Harmony (being at peace with oneself)

Discovering the alignment between your five core values, goals and dreams are vital to your future success. In addition, the beauty about being a Rhino is that you don't have to justify your values, goals or dreams. They are yours! Identify what is important to you and don't judge or crush other Rhino's dreams, visions and goals. Support them and help them in their charge. Lift the positive vibrations in yourself and others by sharing your values, goals and dreams!

RAPID GOAL ACHIEVEMENTS

❑ I learned to eliminate false beliefs about myself.

❑ I broke the 'elephant's chain' of being a prisoner of my own mind.

❑ I understand I am the average of the ten people I spend the most time with.

❑ I am attracting more positive relationships into my life.

❑ I have eliminated the negative people in my life and the negative beliefs about my abilities and negative self-talk.

❑ I have replaced the negative self-talk and beliefs with positive thoughts.

❑ I reframe negative situations into something positive.

❑ I am grateful for what I have been given.

❑ I am committed to living and setting goals aligned with my core values.

❑ I went to RhinoLiving.com and signed up to become a Rhino VIP so I can access free Rhino Action tools for success.

**"ALL THAT WE ARE IS THE RESULT OF
WHAT WE HAVE THOUGHT."**
-Buddha

CHAPTER THREE
WRITE DOWN YOUR GOALS

Write them down and make them S.M.A.R.T.!

Goals should be straight forward and emphasize what you want to happen. S.M.A.R.T. goals focus your efforts and clearly define what you are going to do.

Specific (S) - A specific goal has a much greater chance of being accomplished than a general goal. To set a specific goal you must answer the six "W" questions:

*Who: Who is involved?
*What: What do I want to accomplish?
*Where: Identify a location.
*When: Establish a time frame.
*Which: Identify requirements and constraints.
*Why: Specific reasons, purpose or benefits of accomplishing the goal.

Example: A general goal would be, "Get in shape." But a specific goal would say, "Join a health club and workout 3 days a week."

Measurable (M) - Establish concrete criteria for measuring progress toward the attainment of each goal you set. When you measure your progress, you stay on track, reach your target dates, and experience the exhilaration of achievement that spurs you on to continued effort required to reach your goal.

To determine if your goal is measurable, ask questions such as, "How much?" "How many?" "How will I know when it is accomplished?"

Attainable (A) - When you identify goals that are most important to you, you begin to figure out ways you can make them come true. You develop the attitudes, abilities, skills, and financial capacity to reach them. You begin seeing previously overlooked opportunities to bring yourself closer to the achievement of your goals.

You can attain most any goal you set when you plan your steps wisely and establish a time frame that allows you to carry out those steps. Goals that may have seemed far away and out of reach eventually move closer and become attainable, not because your goals shrink, but because you grow and expand to match them. When you list your goals, you build your self-image. You see yourself as worthy of these goals, and develop the traits and personality that allow you to possess them.

Realistic (R) - To be realistic, a goal must represent an objective toward which you are both willing and able to work. A goal can be both high and realistic; you are the only one who can decide just how high your goal should be. But be sure that every goal represents substantial progress. A high goal is frequently easier to reach than a low one because a low goal exerts low motivational force. Some of the hardest jobs you ever accomplished actually seem easy simply because they were a labor of love.

Your goal is probably realistic if you truly believe that it can be accomplished. Additional ways to know if your goal is realistic is to determine if you have accomplished anything similar in the past or ask yourself what conditions would have to exist to accomplish this goal.

Timely (T) - A goal should be grounded within a time frame. With no time frame tied to it, there is no sense of urgency. If you want to lose 10 pounds, when do you want to lose it by? "Someday" won't work. But if you anchor it within a timeframe, "by May 1st," then you've set your unconscious mind into motion to begin working on the goal.

T can also stand for **Tangible** - A goal is tangible when you can experience it with one of the senses; that is, taste, touch, smell, sight or hearing. When your goal is tangible, you have a better chance of making it specific and measurable.

Establish your Definite Chief Aim

In Napoleon Hill's book, "Think and Grow Rich," he states that "There are no limitations to the mind except those we acknowledge. Both poverty and riches are the offspring of thought."

The Definite Chief Aim comes from the book "Think and Grow Rich ." If you have never read this book, I strongly suggest you pick up a copy right now. It has been one of the most influential books I have ever read!

Creating your Definite Chief Aim is easy. To get started, first answer these three simple questions. I am going to use the example of acquiring money.

1. How much money do you want to acquire?
2. How much time do you want to pass before you have it?
3. What service or plan do you have to acquire it?

The first two questions are easy! Have fun dreaming about how much money you want and how long you are willing to wait to get it. The third question, understandably, takes a little bit more thought.

You must understand that you can't get something for nothing in this world. If you want a million dollars within the next three years, you need to provide a million dollars worth of value within the next three years!

In order to receive, you first have to give! So, think of a service that you can provide for others that people will be willing to pay you for. Actors have the service of entertaining. Inventors have the service of making products that make the customers life easier. Doctors have the service of making you healthier.

What service are you going to provide?

For me, my service is to improve the lives of millions of people through sharing my business knowledge and passion for living a Rhino's life through Rhino Living. I spend a little bit of my time each and every day writing articles and answering emails. I'm trying to make the world a better place by helping others.

Give it some thought. Once you have the three questions from above answered, summarize your answers into a paragraph or two. This is going to be your Definite Chief

Aim. Here is an example similar to the one from the book, "Think and Grow Rich."

"By December 31, [insert year], I will have in my possession $1,000,000, which will come to me in various times during the interim.

In return for this money, I will give the best service that I possibly can in the area of selling. I will… (Describe what you will be doing here.)

I believe I will have this money in my possession. My faith is so strong that I can now see this money in my bank statement. It flows to me more and more with the amount of service I provide."

The third paragraph is important. You have to impress in your mind that you truly believe it is going to happen. The more you believe it is going to happen, the more it is going to work.

This is the real secret behind the Definite Chief Aim!

If you don't believe that you will accomplish what your Definite Chief Aim says, then it isn't going to do anything for you. So give yourself a reasonable amount of time to get your desired amount. That way you will have more belief.

I strongly suggest that you get started on creating your Definite Chief Aim. Once you have 100% belief that you will become a millionaire, your mind starts working in a complete different way. You start doing the things necessary to make yourself rich. You start becoming more observant to wealthy ideas. You start thinking of more and more ways you can earn the figure that you set within your given time frame.

Below define your "SMART" definite chief aims—financial, family, career, and health goals as if they are already a reality! Whatever you think about, consistently and with emotion, will become your eventual reality—positive or negative. Do not restrict your mind in any way. The negative thoughts in your head today are most likely false and have no basis in fact. List your SMART goals in the POSITIVE!

My positive, SMART goals:

Definite Chief Aims for this year:

1. Career Goal:

2. Family Goal:

3. Financial Goal:

4. Health Goal:

Write down your Definite Chief Aim five years from now! *Where you will be in five years is exactly where you think you will be!*

Write down your 3x5 goals

As I always say, achieving a goal is a hands-on project. I will show you what I mean using a 3x5 index card as a goal-setting tool. Keep in mind, you can certainly tweak any suggestions here as you see fit.

I would write down the particular goal. For example, let's say my personal goal is to write at least one new article a week.

I would write the following on my 3x5 index card:

"I write and complete one or more motivational articles a week. I receive nice notes from people that read my writing to let me know that they found the ideas helpful. This or something better is happening in my life now for the good of all concerned."

It's worth noting that I do adjust the wording according to the particular goal I am writing down, but in all instances, I like to include the last part which reads "This or something better is happening in my life now for the good of all concerned."

One of my core values is giving to others. I call it my Give, Serve, Love Philosophy.
Give for the sake of giving.
Serve for the sake of serving.
Love for the sake of loving.

You certainly don't have to add that part, but for me, I find it helps to keep me focused on my larger objective of helping others. Hopefully you also noticed a few other things I like to include on my personal goal cards from the example above.

In case you missed them they are:

1. Write in the present tense.

I find this helps make the distinction in my mind between what I am doing and what I will do or want to do. I want to be active and take real action necessary to experience the results versus simply writing down what I'd like to do. Remember, we're on our way to making our goals a reality. When we take the needed steps to achieving them, we not simply hoping they'll happen on their own. Writing my goals in the present tense makes a difference.

2. Include a little supporting statement for your goal.

In the example above, I included "I receive nice notes from people that read my writing to let me know that they found the ideas helpful." I find that including a statement like this helps to give life to my goal—and help highlight one of the reasons why it is worth taking the effort to work on the goal.

You might consider it written visualization. Just as visualizing an outcome in your mind helps to manifest your goals, so does adding a little written visualization to your goal card will give some added emotion as you are reading and reviewing them.

The key to why keeping your goals written down on 3x5 index cards works is because they're easy to keep around.

They can easily fit in your pocket, on your desk, or practically anywhere. Since it is easy to keep them nearby, it is also easy to review them often! And make no mistake... Reviewing your goals as often as possible is what makes all the difference.

Think of it like this. When it comes to goal achievement, out of sight and out of mind is a killer. And seeing as how our lives can move as fast as the Rhino can charge, it is far too easy to be sidetracked by any number of life's challenges.

So in summary, set regular times with yourself during your day to review your goal cards. Keep them in places where they won't be easily missed. While it is true this idea is a simple one, it is also true that it is easy to neglect taking action on it. While simple, it does work—if you work persistently at the goal!

Create personal vision boards

One of the Laws of the Jungle is The Law of Attraction. In my keynotes, I talk about the importance of creating a "vision board." We've looked before at how powerful it can be to actually write down your goals, and a vision board is sort of a visual representation of these goals. The more clearly you can imagine what you want, the more likely you are to pursue it! This is a matter of making a poster full of images and words that symbolize what you want in life.

A vision board can be a poster-board on which you paste or collage images that you've torn out from various magazines. It's simple. The idea behind this is that when you surround yourself with images of who you want to become, what you want to have, where you want to live, or where you want to vacation, your life changes to match those images and those desires.

I create vision boards with every project, idea, and Definite Chief Aim. It's a ton of fun! Increase positive vibrations and let others get involved in the process. Cut pictures out of magazines, lay out related motivational quotes, people or phrases like "I deserve_____."

This is such a positive way to spend a couple of hours. Once you've completed your vision board, put it somewhere that will allow you to see it often. I've heard of people making it their screen saver on their computer. Mine lives in my office. Looking at it reinforces that these are the things I want in life. Of course, major life changes aren't as simple as making a collage, but it can be a good starting point. Focusing on what you desire helps you to take the steps to attain it. Making choices that lead to a satisfying, fulfilling life is definitely something good!

RAPID GOAL ACHIEVEMENTS

❑ All of my short term goals are S.M.A.R.T.

❑ I established my 'Definite Chief Aim' in the four major areas of my life for one year and five years.

❑ I understand that all success comes from providing service to others. The better the service and the more people I serve, the larger the reward.

❑ I carry my 3x5 goal card with me everywhere I go.

❑ I am passionate about my goals and I believe I can achieve them.

❑ My vision board hangs where I can see it everyday and it inspires me to charge towards my goals.

❑ I shared my goals and progress with people who support my dreams and aspirations.

"OBSTACLES ARE THOSE FRIGHTFUL THINGS YOU SEE WHEN YOU TAKE YOUR EYES OFF YOUR GOAL."
–Henry Ford

CHAPTER FOUR
READ YOUR GOALS TWICE DAILY WITH ENERGY AND ENTHUSIASM

Once you have written your Definite Chief Aim, read it to yourself every night before you go to bed. Then do the same thing when you first wake up.

Every time you read your Definite Chief Aim, you are planting this seed further and further into your subconscious mind. It's your subconscious mind that helps make your dreams a reality.

It has more power than you can ever imagine. After all, this very second your subconscious mind is…

- telling your lungs to breathe
- telling your heart to pump blood
- functioning your organs to digest food

…and so many other things! It works 24 hours a day, 7 days a week.

Giving you the plans and ideas to acquire the wealth you desire is a piece of cake for your subconscious mind. It handles much more difficult tasks on a daily basis!

Here is what I suggest you do…

Read your Definite Chief Aim and 3x5 cards every night before bed and every morning when you wake up with energy and enthusiasm for three weeks. If by then, you don't have more confidence, more belief, and a more optimistic attitude that you will become a millionaire and reach all your goals, then you can stop reading your Definite Chief Aim and 3x5 cards.

I say this because I know it will work for you. I know how much of an impact is it going to have on you. It's going to get you started in the right direction. And it's going to keep pushing you forward every day until one day your Definite Chief Aim will come true. At that point, you won't have to read it anymore. You'll have to get a new one!

Act as if

When I was a chiropractic school, there were motivational quotes all over the place. In a medical world where 90% of people think that drugs and surgeries cure everything, and you are the 10% in the chiropractic world that believes the body heals itself, you definitely need lots of motivation.

This quote always got to me, "Act as if…" Act as if what? What does that mean? Then, after reading success books and going through a few years of practice, it all made sense. It's like the saying, "fake it till you make it." Act as if you are a success and you will be a success. Act positive and you will be positive! Act so if you can't fail and you won't!

"Act as if" is a great attitude and way to charging successfully through life. If you want to be a successful salesperson in two years, act as if you are that person today. Walk, talk and act like you are already that person and you will become what you "act" like. There are many reasons why this is true. For now, focus on the fact that your attitude is the number one key ingredient in your success. Without the right attitude, you cannot charge!

You have already begun to explore all your dreams and passions, and then, just as you are ready to charge, others might say, "that will never work." That's when you charge full steam ahead and "act as if!" That's when you know you can do it! How many people told Edison to give up on the light bulb? How many people told Bill Gates he was crazy to think everyone would have a computer on their desk? How many people told women they didn't have the right to vote? How many people told Ronald Ragan to stay in acting as he could never be President? How many people told a young black senator with a Muslim background he could never be President? Every big dream, big vision, and big goal ever realized had its critics! Tell "those people" to go try and live their dreams instead of squashing yours!

Put your goals on auto pilot

Achieving your goals faster than you ever thought possible becomes very easy when it is "just who you are." Successful people are always successful even in failure. Millionaires and billionaires have gone bankrupt and then in a very short time become wealthy again. The goal seeking success driven personality is so embedded in their subconscious mind that they automatically find ways to achieve wealth even after hitting rock bottom.

Reading your goals aloud with emotion will embed them deep into your subconscious mind. Your goals will simply become who you are. You will walk, talk and act consistent with your dominant goals. Your brain will be programmed to seek out your goals and reaching your goals will become a habit, a habit you don't even need to think about.

The best analogy I can give you is to think for a moment about your dream car. Picture it in your head—the color, the interior, the way you would look and feel driving it. It's easy, isn't it? That dream car is embedded in your brain as an important priority in your life. It is so important that when you see your dream car a block away, a mile away or even flying down the highway at 90 miles an hour, you notice it automatically. You don't even have to think about it. Out of the corner of your eye your subconscious mind notices the car and your brain takes over making it a priority for you to focus on. While you are busy looking and concentrating on all the other busy things going on in your life, your subconscious mind will notice your dream car and draw your attention to it automatically!

Achieving goals faster works the same way. When your subconscious mind becomes deeply programmed with your top goals is because it is always working on them. Even when you are busy dealing with paperwork, emails, and meetings, your subconscious mind is always observing your environment, looking for ways to get you to your goals. Let's say for example that you want to build a shopping center. You have the land, but you are looking for a development partner. While you are busy at the airport buying a coffee and a magazine and about to board a plane, your subconscious mind picks up on a conversation between two guys a few feet away. Your subconscious mind hears them discussing land deals and it automatically pulls your attention away from the coffee and magazine transaction to something much more important to you. The next thing you know you have met your land developer and 6 months later your shopping center is open all with very little effort. Your subconscious mind did all the work while you were busy buying a coffee.

When you are auto programmed to achieve success, you are always working towards your goals. Napoleon Hill says, "Whatever the mind can conceive and believe, it can achieve." Your brain is always alert for opportunities to help you achieve your top priorities. It occurs when you are working, sleeping or even on vacation. A successful, goal seeking Rhino is just who you are therefore opportunities are always being brought to your attention this is why successful people can accomplish amazing things in a very short period of time.

Go the extra mile

Once you have programmed your mind for success reaching your goals will require much less effort. If you want to increase the speed at which you reach your goals even more, then put this next principle into action. Go the extra mile with every client, guest, employee, and employer -- essentially every relationship you have. When you go the extra mile and put more energy out than is required you will always get a bigger return.

If you want to get paid more in the future you need to

start doing more today. You will always be compensated in proportion of the energy you give out. Don't expect to get more business, a promotion or a new opportunity if you are doing just enough to get by. If you want a six figure income you need to deliver six figures worth of service now, not later. Putting forth the quality and service associated with a lower value will keep you at a lower level of success. When you start to provide more and better service than is expected of you then you start to experience the rewards of your efforts.

We need you to lead

BJ Palmer said, "Make your decision for what is right, not expedient. Wash your mind of all compromise." Everywhere in society we need strong determined leaders to help us create a better world. We need Rhino leaders in all businesses, civic organizations and every aspect of our society and we need them now! We need true Rhinos to step up and start taking charge to make this world a better place.

Rhino leaders look to create long-term success. They don't follow the easy path or the clear path. They follow the right path to create the right solutions. Rhino leaders need to take charge in the political world immediately. We need Rhino politicians to resist the temptations of special interests and short-term gains to secure our future. We all know there is no such thing as clean coal—it's impossible! We need a leader to stand up and say, "to make Green energy work, it means we need different cars and different homes and we need to make sacrifices… as a result, in 20 years we will all still have a planet to live on."

The problem with most leaders today is they lead by opinion polls. Opinion polls only register the individual concerns of voters. The most important opinion a person has is based on how something will affect them. If you work for or own a coal company, of course you will vote for coal even if you know it's wrong. We need Rhino leaders who realize the tough decisions must be made now to benefit future generations and that means the current generations will simply have to adapt—it's part of life.

If every leader took time to read this statement before making any important decision, the world would be a very different place. You are a natural leader. You may not even know it yet, but you are. If you signed up for the Rhino emails, it means you are different than the majority of the population. It means you are striving to achieve your goals and to make a difference. It means you want to transcend your mediocre life to create an incredible life.

Well, that incredible life comes with Rhino responsibilities! You need to lead others down the path of a better life. You need to make hard decisions and sometimes stand alone defending an unpopular truth. You need to charge full steam ahead when everyone is begging you to stop.

With your company, your employees, your coworkers and your family, you need to be the person that stands out and takes a stand for the best long-term decisions and demonstrate best long-term leadership. You need to resist the grazing temptations of taking the politically correct or safe path.

We are in the mess we are today because of watered down

leadership. We need you to take a stand and show people how it can be done. And don't think I'm crazy—even Lee Iacocca agrees with me in his phenomenal book "Where Have All the Leaders Gone." A definite must read for every Rhino!

Starting from this point forward, I challenge you to take the Rhino Road to leadership!

1. Set high Rhino standards for any project you are working. Refuse to take the cow path and follow the rest of the herd. Refuse to compromise your Rhino values and qualities.

2. Don't represent the dreams and ideals for the special interests of the world. Be a role model for others and charge towards a better future through every Rhino action. Remember following the path of least resistance makes men, women and rivers crooked.

3. Be a true Rhino in all your business dealings. Create win-win deals and look to build true relationships in your business dealings.

4. Go the extra mile and give more than you receive.

5. Finally, stand up and defend the truth even when everyone else is pretending to be blind with ignorance— whether it is in your home, your company, your congress or your church or synagogue.

Charge forward Rhino Leaders!

RAPID GOAL ACHIEVEMENTS

- ❏ I read my goals twice daily with energy and enthusiasm. My subconscious mind will make success a habit.
- ❏ 'Act as if'… as if you are the success you want to become. Walk the walk, talk the talk, become who you want to be.
- ❏ I realize tough decisions are necessary and sometimes a leader stands alone in achieving goals.
- ❏ I will take action daily to achieve my goals. The more positive energy I put out towards my goals, the more success I will achieve.

"LEADERS ARE VISIONARIES WITH A POORLY DEVELOPED SENSE OF FEAR AND NO CONCEPT OF THE ODDS AGAINST THEM. THEY MAKE THE IMPOSSIBLE HAPPEN."
–Robert Jarvik

STEP FIVE:
TAKE ACTION, PERSIST AND ADAPT

Success Comes from Charging through Failures and Towards Goals

Top Rhinos will make mistakes. The more audacious your goals, the bigger your potential failures and mistakes could be! The point to remember is that mistakes are the foundations of success. You cannot be successful without having a string of failures in your past. Full grown Rhino's understand this and realize that charging on and learning from the big and small failures is how you will become a huge success.

The foundation of my Rhino Living Philosophy is a positive mental attitude. A positive attitude and a positive world and life view will keep your failures in perspective. A positive attitude will keep you focused on learning from your mistakes and it will help you maintain momentum as you charge towards your goals. I challenge you to use setbacks as launching pads for your charge and look at it as failing forward.

There are two ways to look at the world—the benevolent way or the pessimistic way. A person with a pessimistic world view takes a victim stance, seeing life as unfair, seeing the world oppressing them and observing nothing but obstacles, preventing a happy, successful life. These people expect problems and misery and that's exactly what they get! This describes two main Laws of the

Jungle—the Law of Attraction and the Law of Cause and Effect. You attract things and people into your life often because of the things you do that attracts them—both good and bad! They see the world as hostile, negative and unfair. As a result, their perception creates their reality.

Rhinos have positive worldview. They see the world around them as filled with opportunities and possibilities. They look for the positive in all situations and they focus on positive events rather than negative setbacks. Most importantly, they see the universe as benevolent, conspiring to do good and help them achieve great things. The benevolent universe approach helps the Rhino charge relentlessly at their dreams because they know that by following the four Laws of the Jungle—including the Law of Cause and Effect, Law of Attraction, Law of Persistence and the Law of Abundance—the world will provide exactly what they need when they need it. It may not appear that everything is going to plan, but a true Rhino knows if they continue to charge towards the right solution, the right rewards will present themselves. Rhinos approach their lives, their work, and their relationships with optimism, and a general attitude of positive expectations. They expect a lot of themselves and others and are seldom disappointed.

I own ten restaurants, have six under construction, two under contract, employ 800 employees and growing, and am launching two new restaurant brands. I also own a moving company with 12 trucks and 50 employees. At the same time, my speaking and writing career has taken off. So during an economy when no one is going out to eat, no one is moving and corporations have cut training and speakers, I am running three businesses directly in the crossfire of this disaster! This just shows you that I could concentrate on the negative economy and all the challenges that come with it, or try to do something about it and charge forward, creating jobs and opportunities for others up and down the east coast. Why would I do this? Because I understand the Rhino Living Philosophy and live it every day—it works! I believe in myself, my abilities, and know this economy too will pass. The key in these bad times is to not lose faith in yourself. You need to continue charging like a Rhino and eliminate all negative thoughts about the past. Let your past failures go, learn from them and move on!

The time is now to take action, Rhinos! In the last chapter I discussed what you have to do—now do it! Your grazing tendencies might return, but if you have been following the checklists and completing the activities in the book, you should be primed to ready to achieve your goals and charge towards your dreams! Next, determine the prize! Determine what great things you can reward yourself with when you achieve your goals. If it's a promotion you seek, plan a weekend trip for when you achieve it. Make it special and important to you!

You need to get out there and make your success happen. Go the extra mile in everything you do. It increases your success and your returns. It's one thing to write your goals down, another to believe you can achieve them, and it's an entirely different process to actually get up early, work late and take action every single day towards your goals. The universe rewards action. Don't whine, don't complain, don't look at the obstacles. Focus on your goals and charge until they are yours.

Rhino prioritization and adaptation in the Jungle of Life

It is important to remember that there might be a need to do some Rhino prioritization and adaptation in the Jungle of Life. Set a time to analyze, clarify and solidify your 'Definite Chief Aim' you set in the last chapter throughout the year. I am constantly adapting, taking on more opportunities and managing people and things that try to take me off my charge—often daily. It can become overwhelming if you don't have a system or plan to handle prioritization and adaptation.

I recommend assessing where you are in your Rapid Goal Achievement process at least four times a year. You might want to do it with the change of the seasons. Make a meeting with yourself! It's symbolic to the changes you might need to make within your plan or what you need to change within yourself. This shift in the seasons will also help you re-channel and re-focus on what you consider important projects, goals and issues. It will also help you eliminate wasteful activities and grazing tendencies that could be taking you off your charge and not allowing you achieve your dreams as fast as you could be.

Strengthen charging forces and weaken grazing forces

As you take action, persist and adapt, it is important to always be searching for ways to strengthen not only your charging traits, but also your charging forces. What's the difference? Traits are found within you. Forces come from the outside. What alliances do you need to build, who is serving you well, and what small wins can you accomplish that will add up to big wins over time? These are all important questions to ask and charge towards. It is just as important to look at the grazing forces that could take you off your charge. Look at how you can weaken them as you charge towards your goals. Don't allow people and situations to take you off your charge. You are a full grown 6,000 pound Rhino with 6 inch skin. You are unstoppable!

A Rhino has survived because it has adapted while every other animal even remotely similar to the Rhino is extinct. The unstoppable charge of the Rhino is what has kept him alive. Nothing can stop the persistent charge of the Rhino. Remember, the natural Law of Persistence as you take action and charge. Persistence in the face of adversity will create amazing results. To give you a glimpse into my life this year, I was in the middle of a major transition in one of my companies. At one time I was dealing with several major life changing decisions.

My to-do list looked like this:
• Sell one of my brands to a national company
• Raise three million in equity to continue to grow the brand
• Open four new units before end of 2009
• Launch new concept, Harvest
• Launch another new concept, MAS Mexicali Cantina
• Launch Rhino Living nationwide
• Write a book
• Buy new beach house; sell old beach house

...and the list goes on!

Selling one of my restaurant brands to a national company was the biggest possible decision with the largest financial pay day but was it time? The economy was in the toilet, banks weren't lending money, and consumers were not going out to dinner. The restaurant industry had its worst year in 28 years. Selling now would be getting out at the bottom, not at the top. Eventually I knew the economy would turn around and the values of restaurants would be much bigger than in this bad economy. The entire purchase process became very crazy. At times it seemed like the entire process and company might implode. At times we had no money for bank debt payments, payroll and even food to supply our restaurants.

Did I panic? No! Success comes in peaks and valleys. This was definitely a valley for one of my brands. At the end, I decided not to sell the brand. I felt it was a difficulty I could charge through. I continued to charge with a big smile on my face! I greeted every employee, vendor, banker and lawyer with a big reassuring smile on my face. I kept my Mercedes shiny clean and acted as if everything was going according to plan.

Every day we worked to increase sales and guest traffic. We hired better management and we improved the value of our brand. Within three short months all our units were up in sales and some units increased sales as much as 25 percent! In the slow summer months we actually broke our previous sales and profit records! And in the process, I actually bought a restaurant off of one of the companies that was looking to buy my company because they ended up in financial hardship. Success can happen that fast. You can be looking at failures and three months later you can be up in sales and expanding your brand. During that time others might have thought I was nuts, but I continued to "act as if" and persisted towards my Definite Chief Aim with unwavering faith that I could achieve my goals.

I expected the problems, the delays, and I knew eventually the right solution would present itself. As a Rhino, I knew I had to persist despite people losing faith in me, despite the economy being hell and despite the fact that it might all implode. A Rhino persists and adapts to the situations around him. A Rhino doesn't curse the darkness, he lights another candle. One door closes and another one opens. The minute you quit, when you say it can't be done, then and only then, are you finished. You and only you choose to fail. You have not failed until you decide to not get back up. Remember, you are an unstoppable iron-plated Rhino, so get back up and charge!

Nobody said success would be easy. You need to expect and prepare for the dark days and for the times when you think it could all implode. The biggest success can be right around the corner. When you have fallen from the peak of success into the dark valley of despair, it is hard to focus on success and the value of your dreams. However, that is exactly what the most successful people in the world do in the face of adversity. When you are in the valley of perceived failure you could start the charge uphill to the highest peak you have ever experienced. Persist and adapt is the Rhino way of life. It is what separates moderate success from giant success!

Remember Charlie's Swindoll's quote I have at the beginning of the book, "life is 10% what happens to me and 90% of how I react to it. And so it is with you... we are in charge of our attitudes." Post it and read it daily!

Now get out there and achieve **BIGGER, BETTER, MORE EXCITING GOALS...FASTER!**

LIVE THE LIFE YOU WERE INTENDED TO LIVE!

RAPID GOAL ACHIEVEMENTS

- ❑ I will take action when my plan is 80% done. No plan is ever 100% perfect.
- ❑ I wake up every day looking for positive opportunities and take action towards them.
- ❑ I persist through the small and large setbacks. The biggest obstacles provide the greatest success.
- ❑ I surround myself with intelligent positive people that inspire me to charge at my dreams.
- ❑ I commit to following my passions. I adapt my plans and persist based on my passionate five-year 'Definite Chief Aim.'

"FAITH IS TAKING THE FIRST STEP EVEN WHEN YOU DON'T SEE THE WHOLE STAIRCASE."
–Martin Luther King, Jr.

ACKNOWLEDGEMENTS

Writing a book is an exciting adventure. Especially when you write the book, edit the book and send it to print in ten days. The energy, passion and excitement drive the creative process day and night.

I look at life as a wonderful adventure full of opportunities to meet wonderful people and live exciting dreams. First, I would like to thank my family for their support and understanding of living with a Rhino 24 hours a day. My beautiful, intelligent daughters, Ivy and Hope, and my amazing little boy, Grady, have to share their father with a lot of people and a lot of businesses. My wife Shannon, who lives a Rhino life of epic proportions. My sister Carolyn and my Aunt Mary Anne for their guidance, wisdom and ability to anchor me when needed.

My close friends, colleagues and mentors have always been there to encourage me to live my dreams and to celebrate success. They have been there for me in good times and bad. A special thanks to Pat Croce, John DeBella, John Caulfield, Mike Rody, Dale Kilgariff, Elana Grande, Caesar Augustus, and Patrick McBride.

My Kildare's and Doc's team of non-stop Rhinos that keep up with my crazy dreams and visions deserve a BIG thank you! Their dedication allows me time to write, speak and travel the country. Thank you Frank Kasper, Frank Daly, Adam Gottlieb, Luke Ainsile, Bill Shewen, Dane and Stephanie Gray.

A special thank you to my Rhino Living team of Molly Nece, Dan Murphy and Allie Harris. Their attention to detail and knowledge of my personality is amazing. It creates wonderful results and an exciting Rhino adventure!

To all the writers and speakers that share their wisdom and knowledge and have provided a wonderful philosophy of living your goals and dreams. To Scott Alexander, the original Rhino, who's book Rhinoceros Success, was the catalyst of my charge back in Chiropractic School. To Jack Canfield, Mark Victor Hansen, Larry Winget, and Napoleon Hill for creating a foundation for me to build this Rhino Living Philosophy.

And finally a very big thank you to the thousands of Rhinos that are part of our RhinoLiving.com Tribe. Your success stories, thank you notes, and messages of inspiration are helping to create a world full of Rhinos!

DR. DAVE MAGROGAN

In six short years, Dave Magrogan took Kildare's from an unknown start up pub to being recognized as the 7th best Irish pub in the world. He is CEO of a $25 million dollar empire—including Rhino Living Training & Consulting Group, Kildare's, Doc Magrogan's Oyster House, Harvest, and Mas Mexicali Cantina. He also serves as president of the Southeastern Pennsylvania Division of Two Men and a Truck Moving Company and helped launch Pat Croce's Rum Barrel in Key West and various other businesses.

Dave has been a finalist in the 2006 and 2007 Ernst & Young Entrepreneur of the year competition. He was also recognized by the Philadelphia Business Journal as one of the region's "40 Under 40" in 2007 and by the Chester County Chamber of Business and Industry as its 2007 Entrepreneur of the Year. He also received the Small Business Administration's Entrepreneurial Success Award for 2008, and Kildare's Irish Pub was ranked 26th in Philadelphia's Fastest growing 100 Companies. Not bad for someone 36 years of age!

Dave has 20+ years of experience in the restaurant industry and holds a Chiropractic Doctorate. He made his first million by building two of the largest family practices in Delaware County, Pennsylvania, where he personally treated over 800 patients a week.

Dave's ultimate goal is to open 25 restaurants up and down the I-95 corridor and leave his legacy of 'Give. Love. Serve.' and continue to inspire his tribe of Rhinos to live and monetize their dreams. Dave attributes his success to living a Rhino's life— jumping in full steam ahead and in a short period of time, accomplishing his set goals. Because of his success and his ability to motivate others, Dave enjoys training businesses, organizations and schools throughout the nation on how to put into action his Rhino Living philosophy—including his 800 staff members! Dave is constantly writing new blogs, emails, books and training materials which can be found on Rhinoliving.com.

When Dave is not in his corporate headquarters and hometown of West Chester, Pennsylvania, he is on the road opening restaurants, developing new brands, or speaking across the globe. Occasionally, he can be found taking Rhino vacations and writing his next book at his home in Key West, Florida or Sea Isle City, New Jersey.

MOLLY NECE

Molly Nece attributes much of her success to her positive mental outlook, her assertiveness and her Legacy Dream Team. Through her coaching, consulting and production company, Legacy Producers, she's been able to help people discover their legacy, find fulfillment in life and share their legacy with others to the Nth degree! Molly also serves as President of Rhino Living and CEO of MyInternshipGopher.com. If that wasn't enough, she is also West Chester University's Senior Internal Consultant.

Molly always goes the extra mile no matter what project she takes on. She also looks for a fit within her personal mission—Make a difference. Be the difference! The Last Sermon Project and Legacy Lecture Program are both great examples of her dedication to living her legacy and fulfilling that mission.

Molly learned early in life that her passion was guiding people to find their full potential and giving them the skills they need to be successful in life. Her higher education career varied from a small private liberal arts women's college in Pittsburgh, a highly selective private liberal arts college in Gettysburg to a large state university in West Chester, Pennsylvania. After spending most of her career in higher education, Wells Fargo Educational Financial Services recruited her into sales and marketing. Although a Rhino sales and marketing superstar, she felt unfulfilled.

Molly said good-bye to the corporate world and completed of her Masters in Training and Organizational Development at West Chester University and received her Lean Six Sigma Certificate from Villanova University. Shortly after, she was asked to join West Chester's Office of Training and Organizational Development.

Over the past 10 years, she's been able to design and deliver over hundreds of professional development training programs, and has inspired tens of thousands of students, faculty, staff, and external organizations, and coached and consulted hundreds of business leaders and their front lines. Molly is committed to making a difference in the lives of others and helping them live their legacy they were intended to leave!